Health and Safety

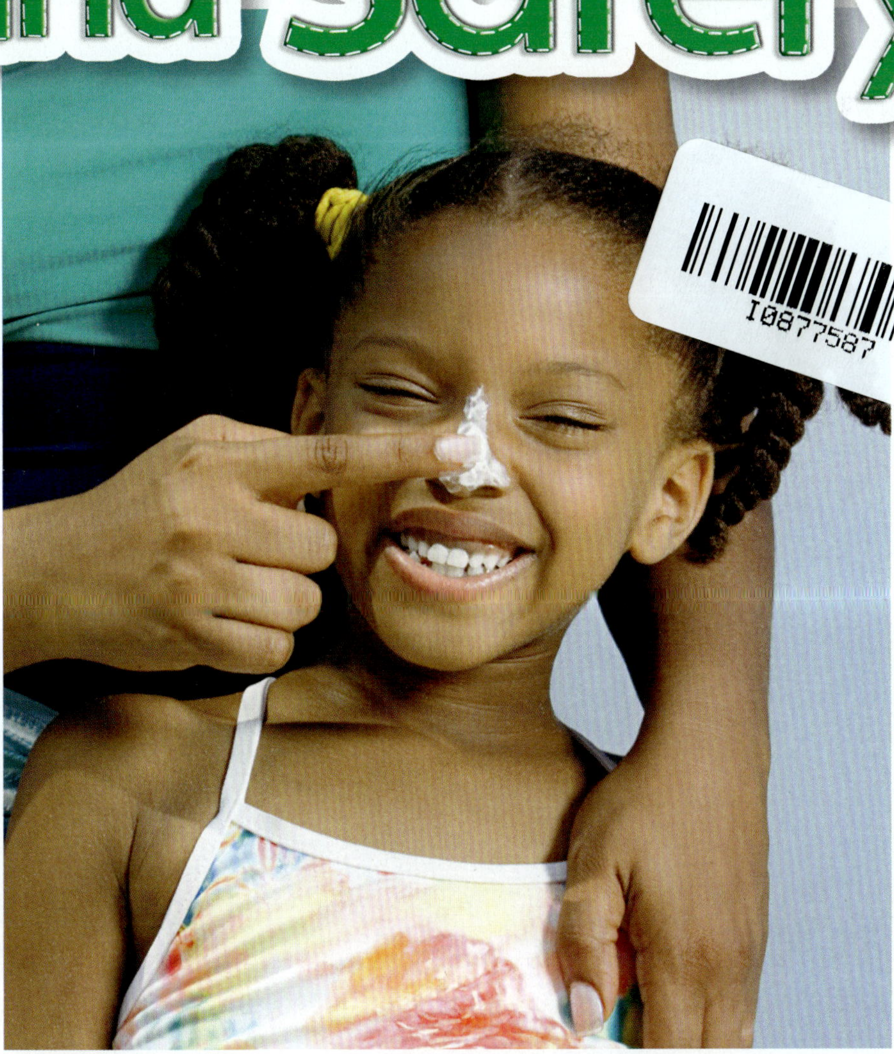

Stephanie Reid

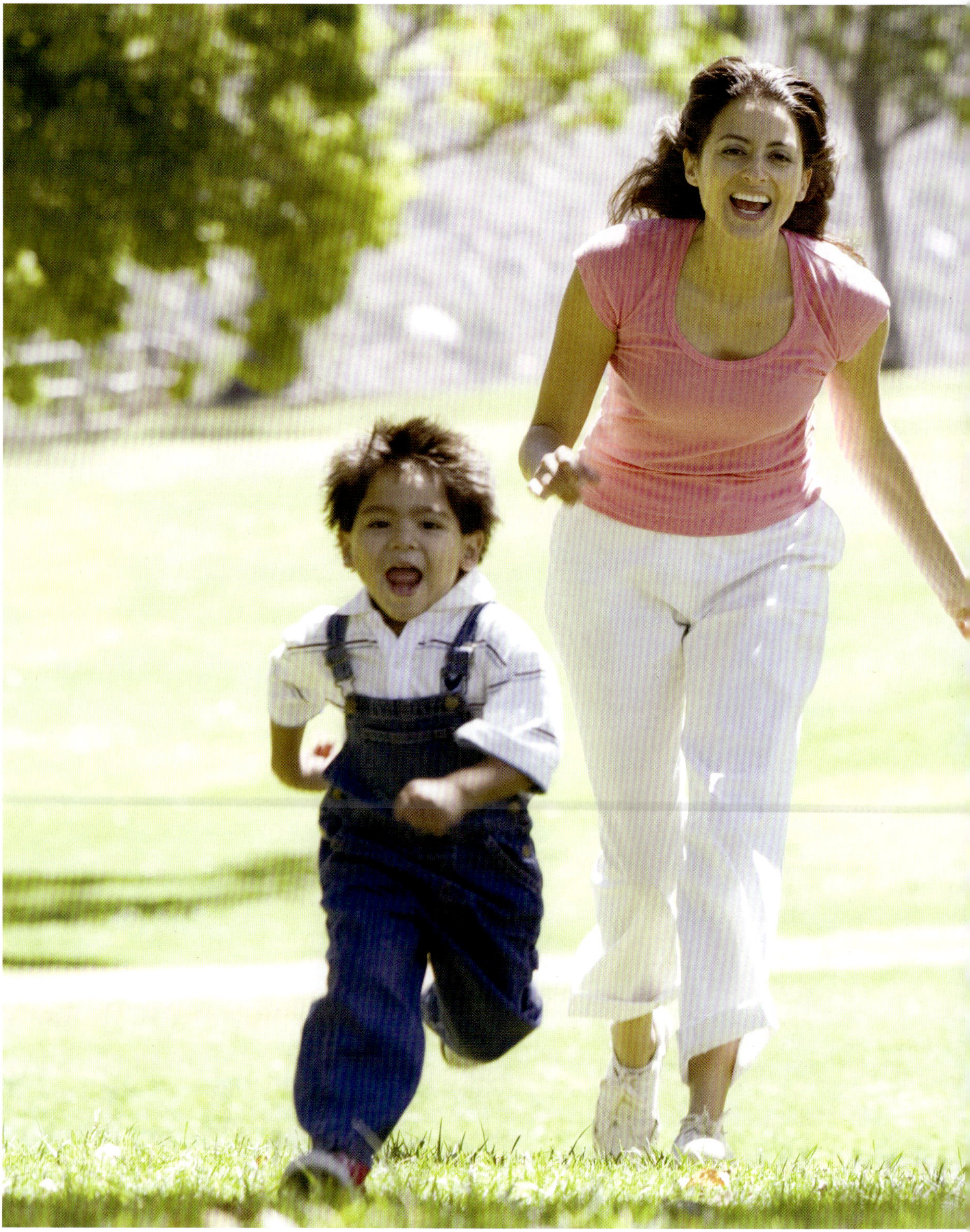

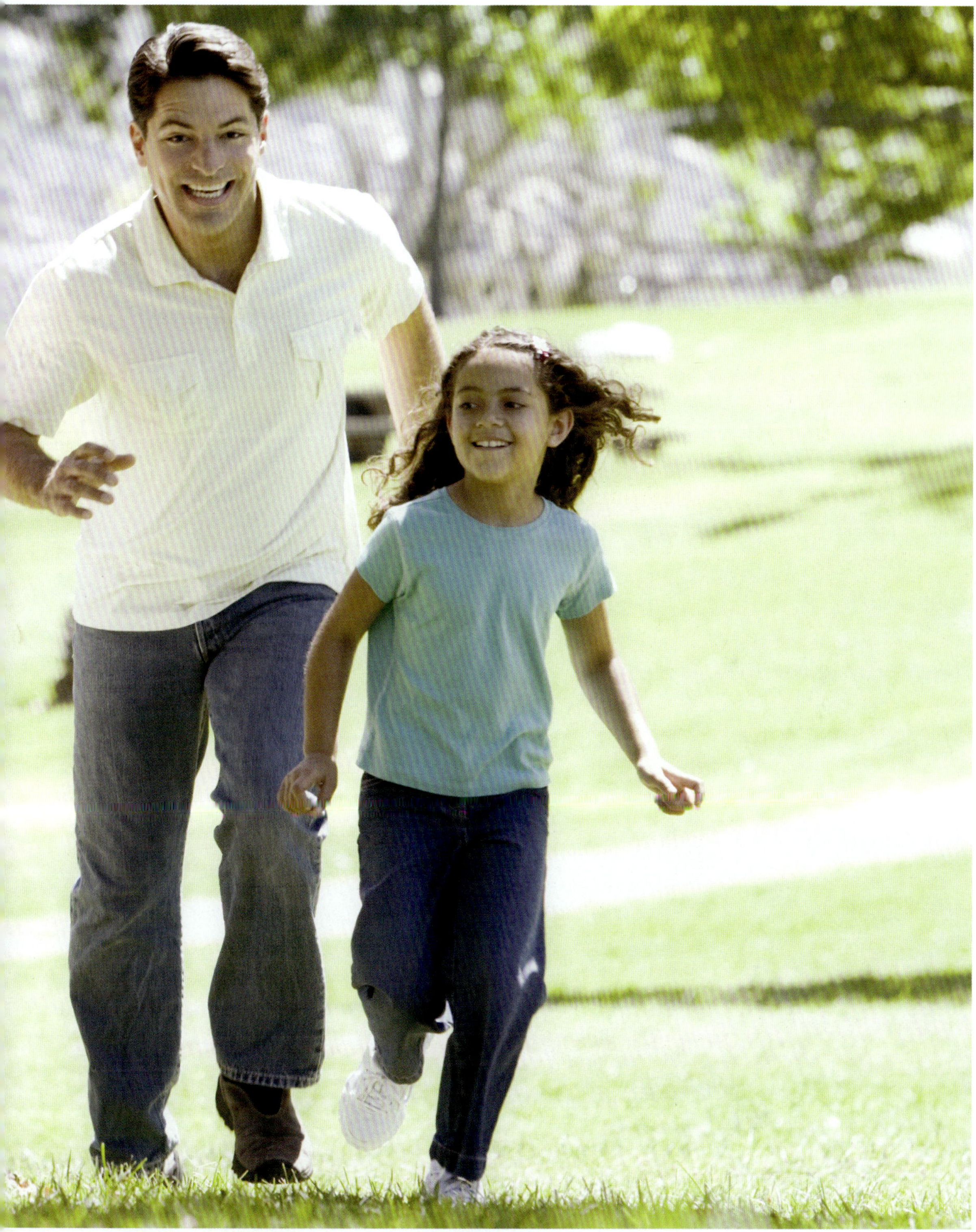

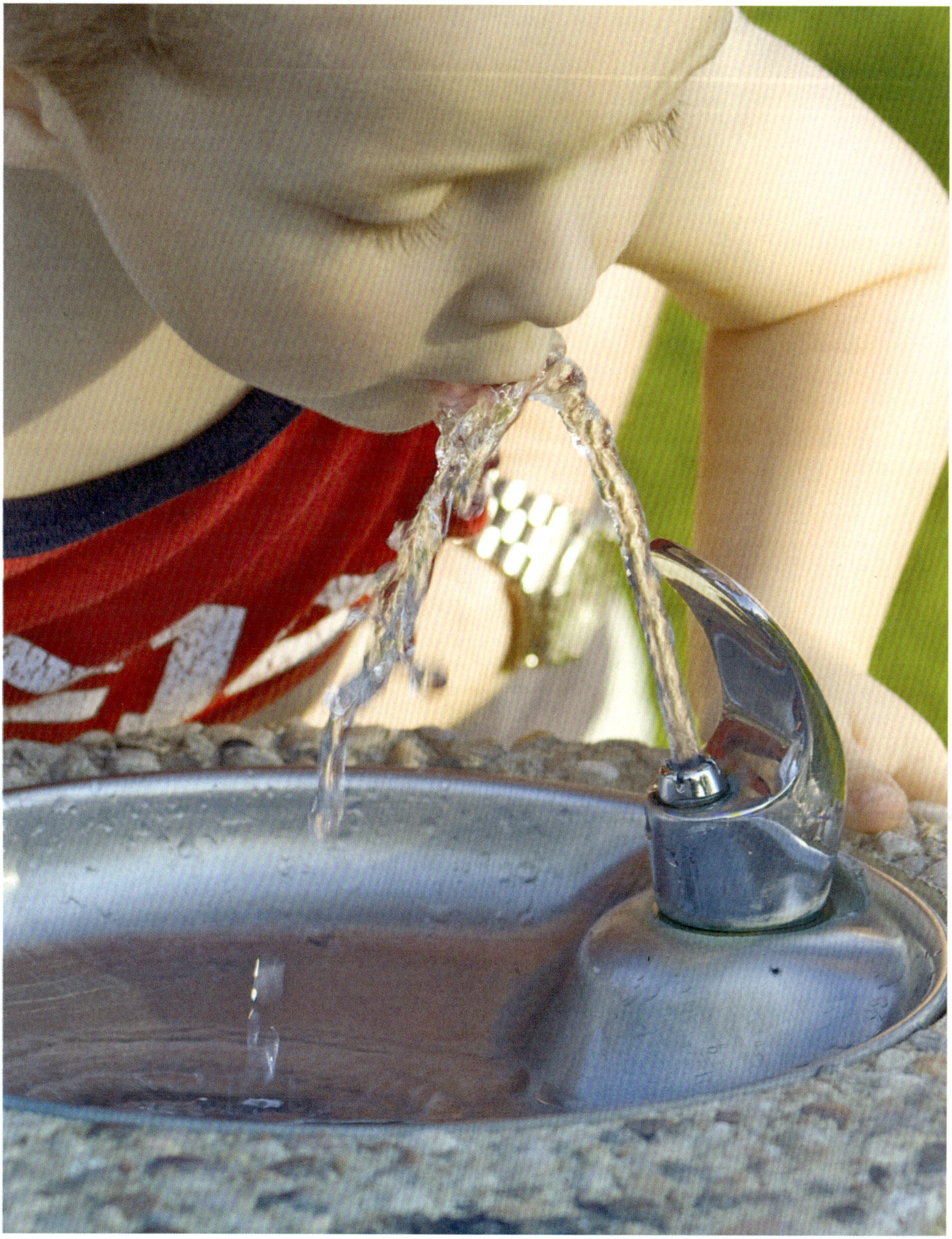

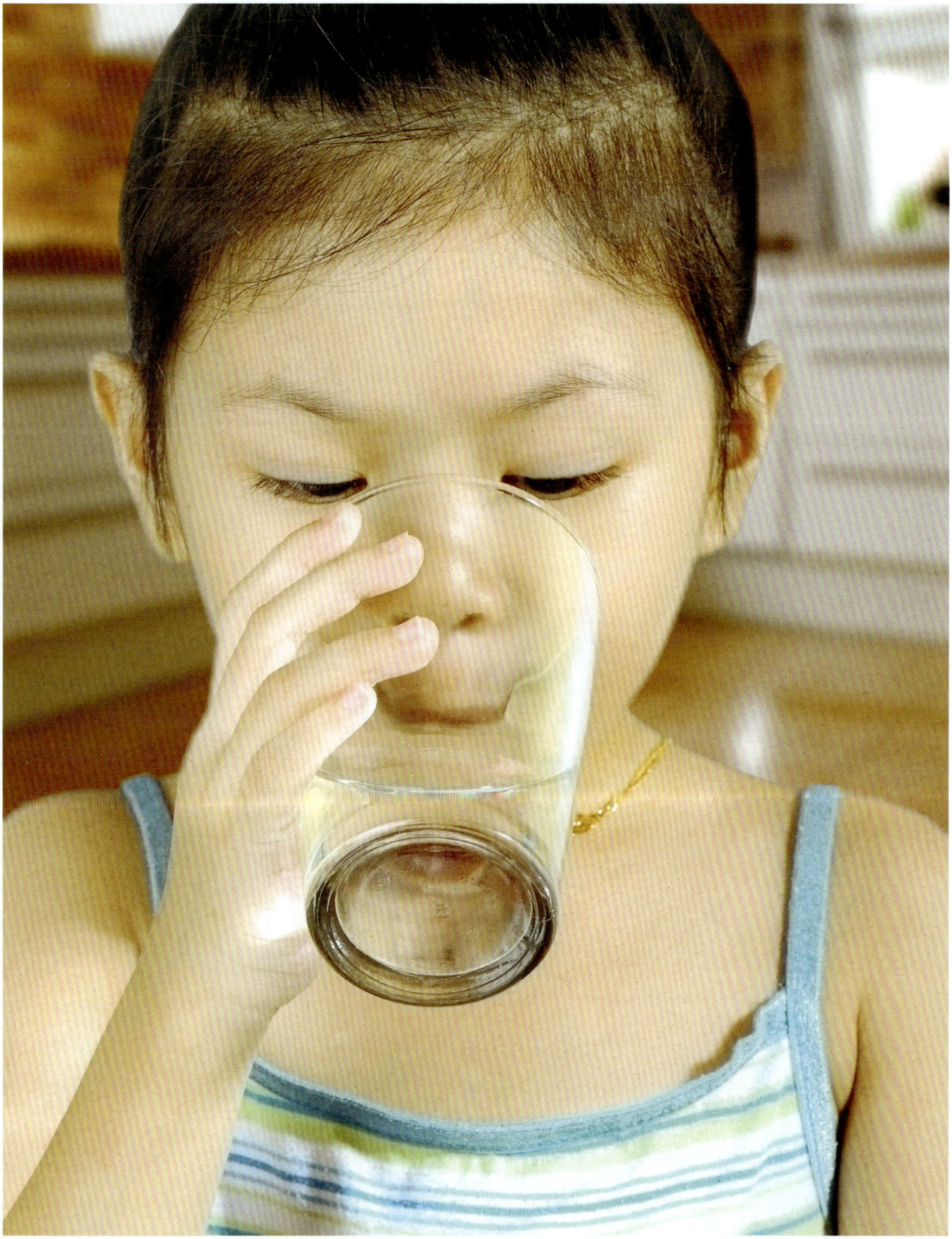

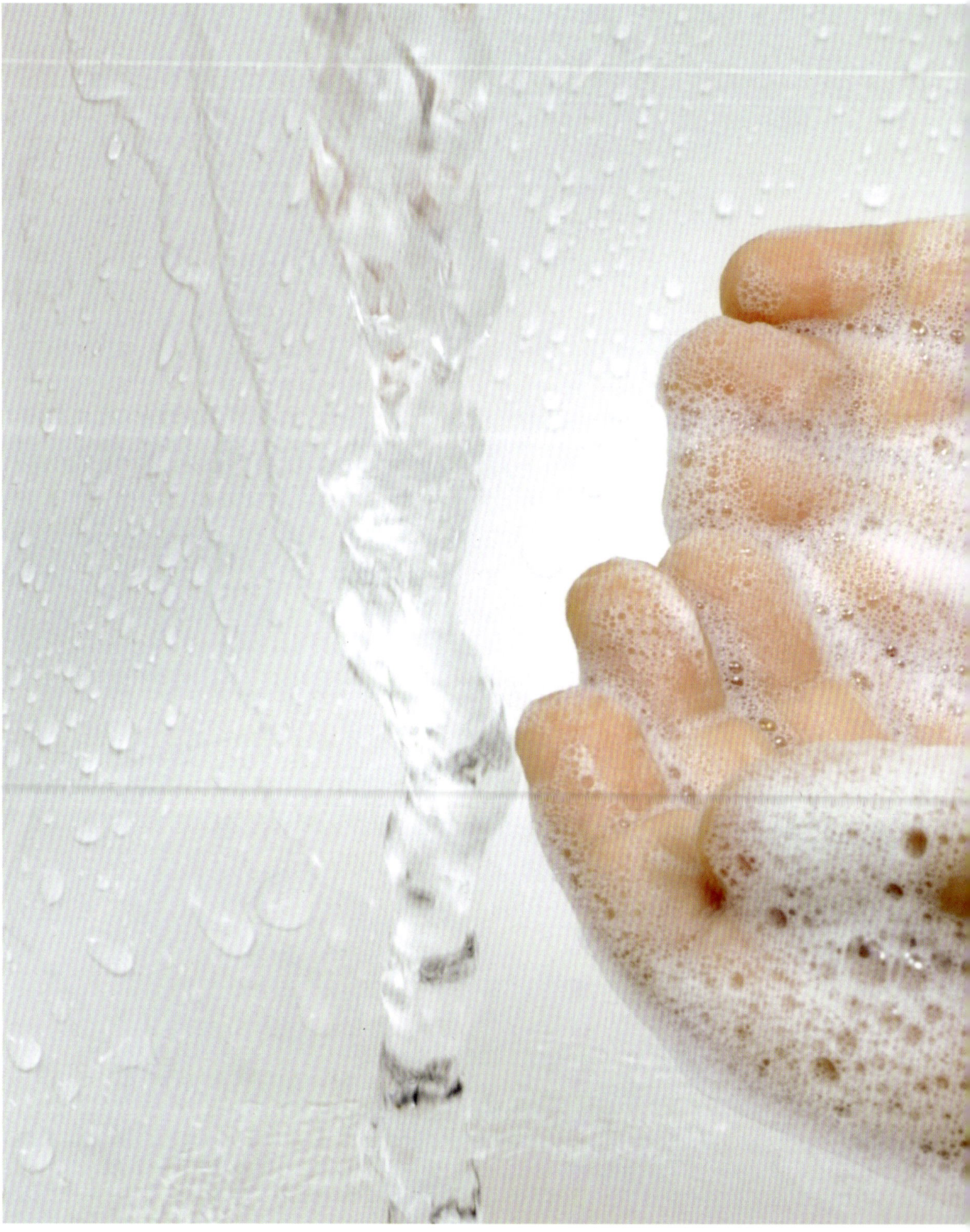

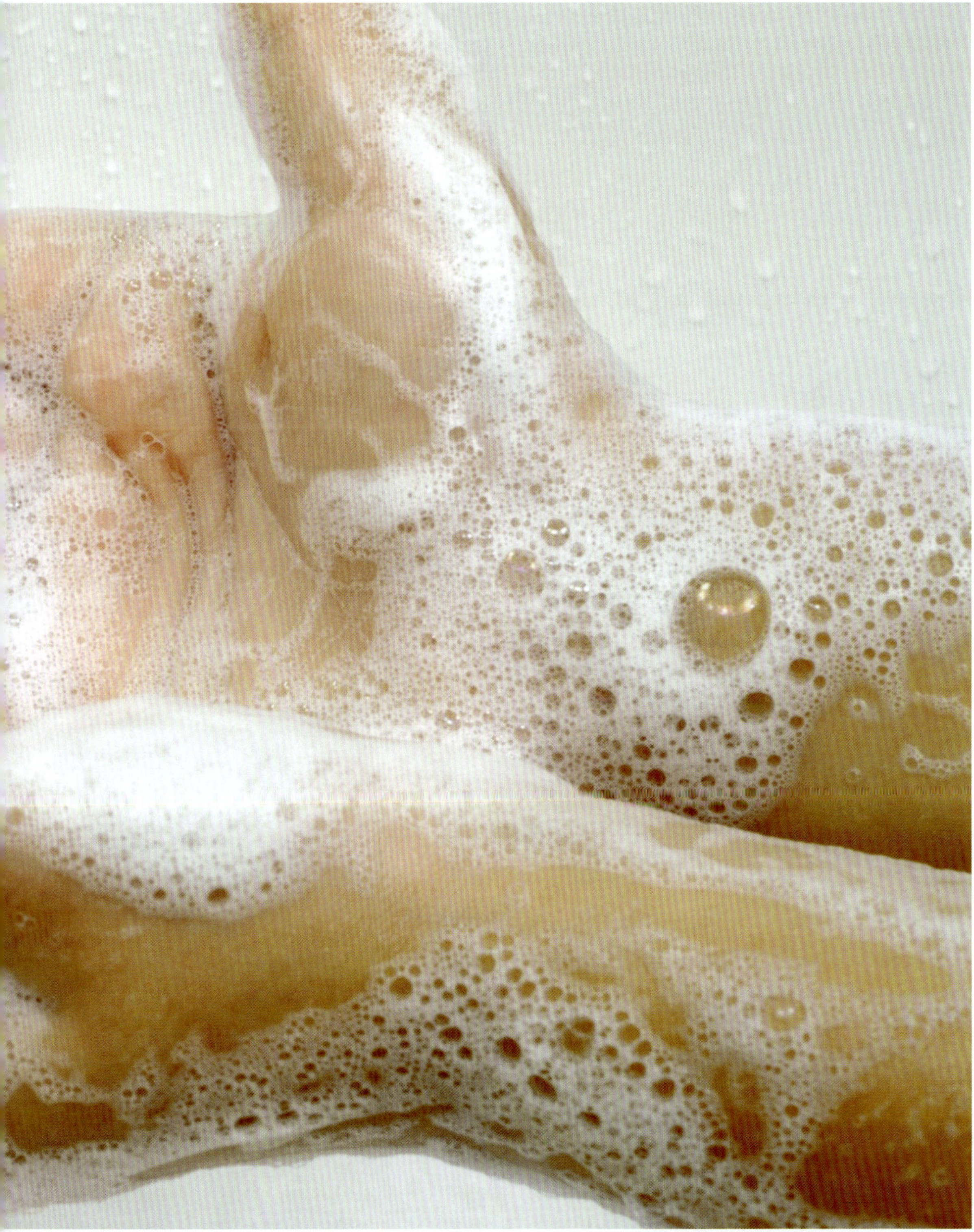

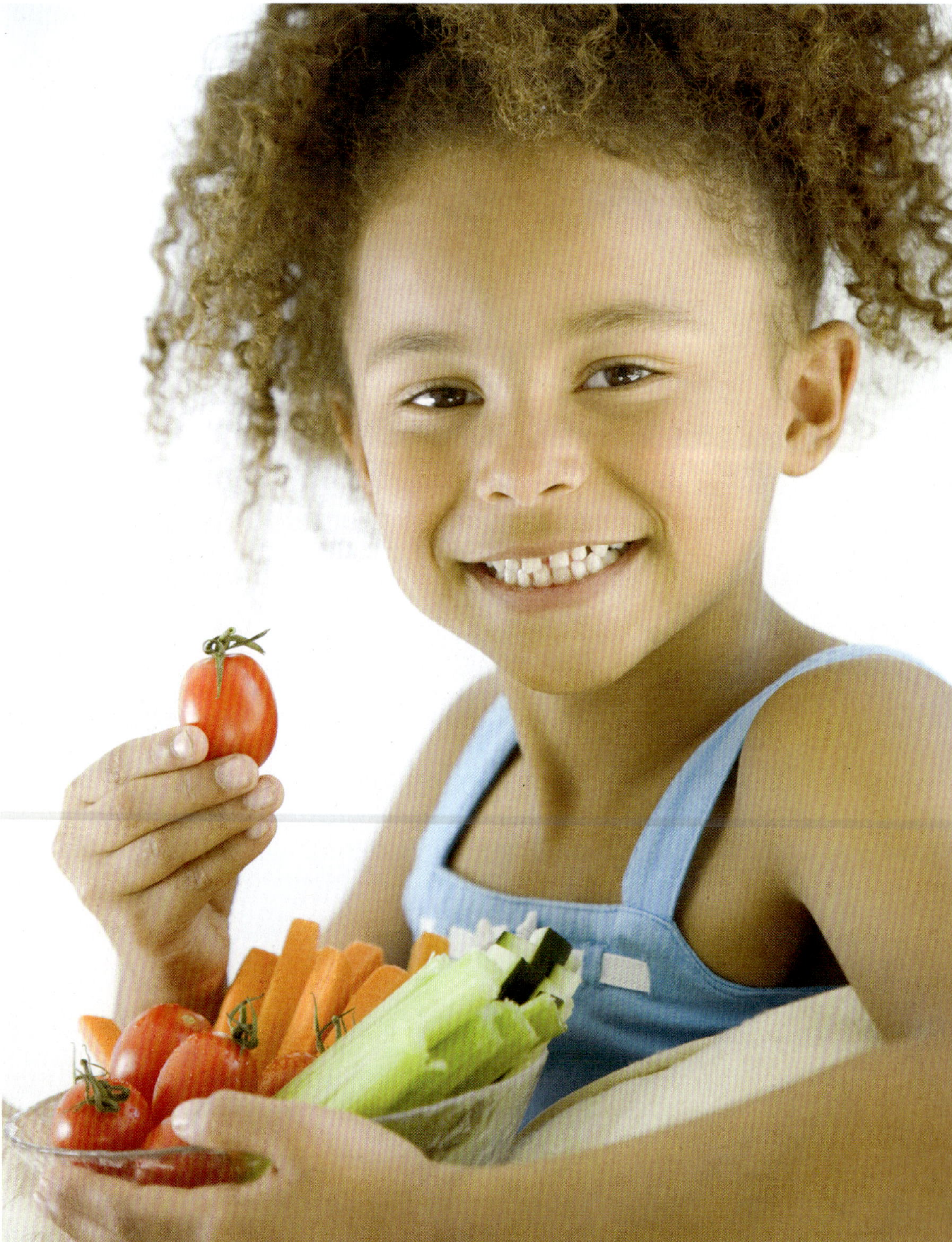

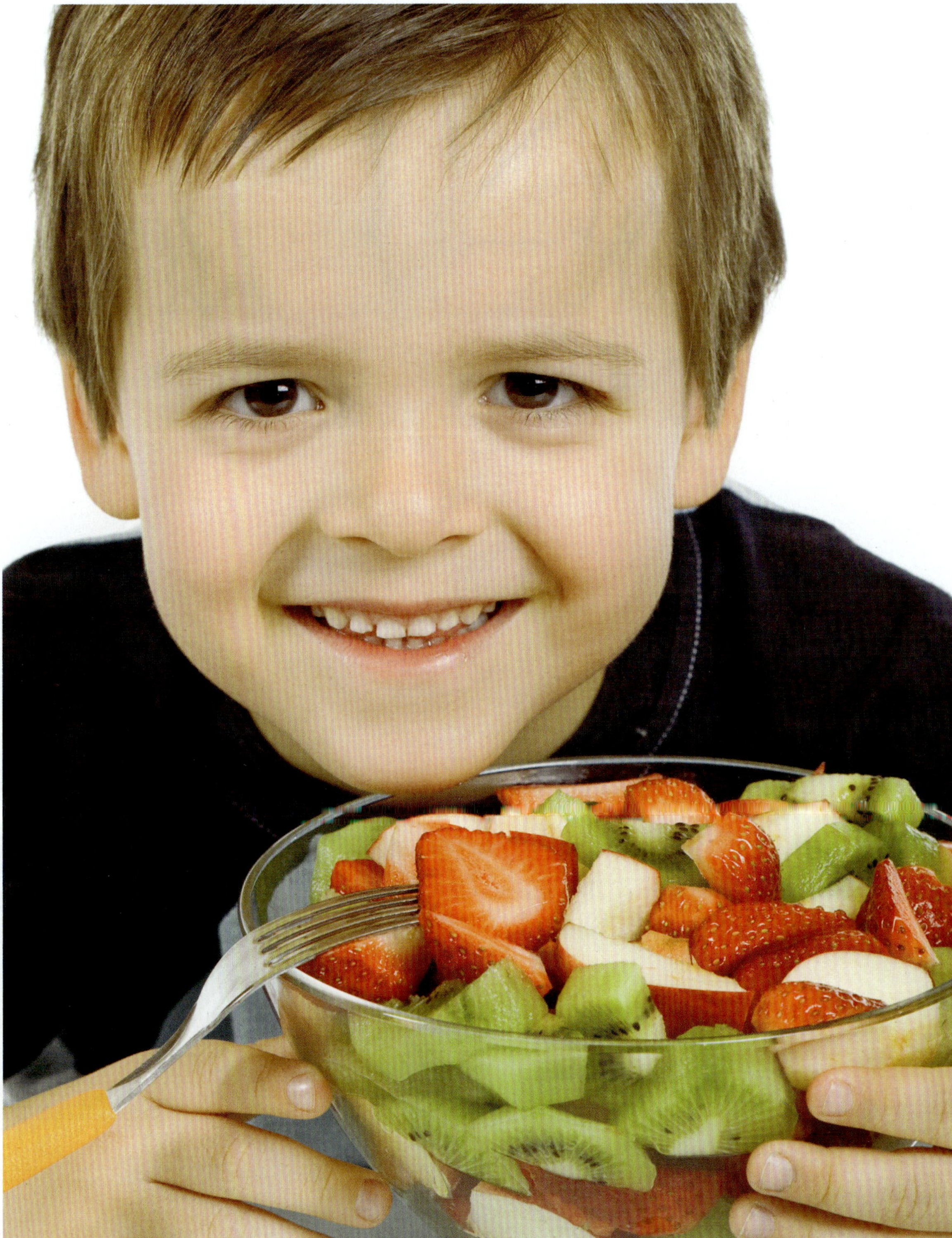

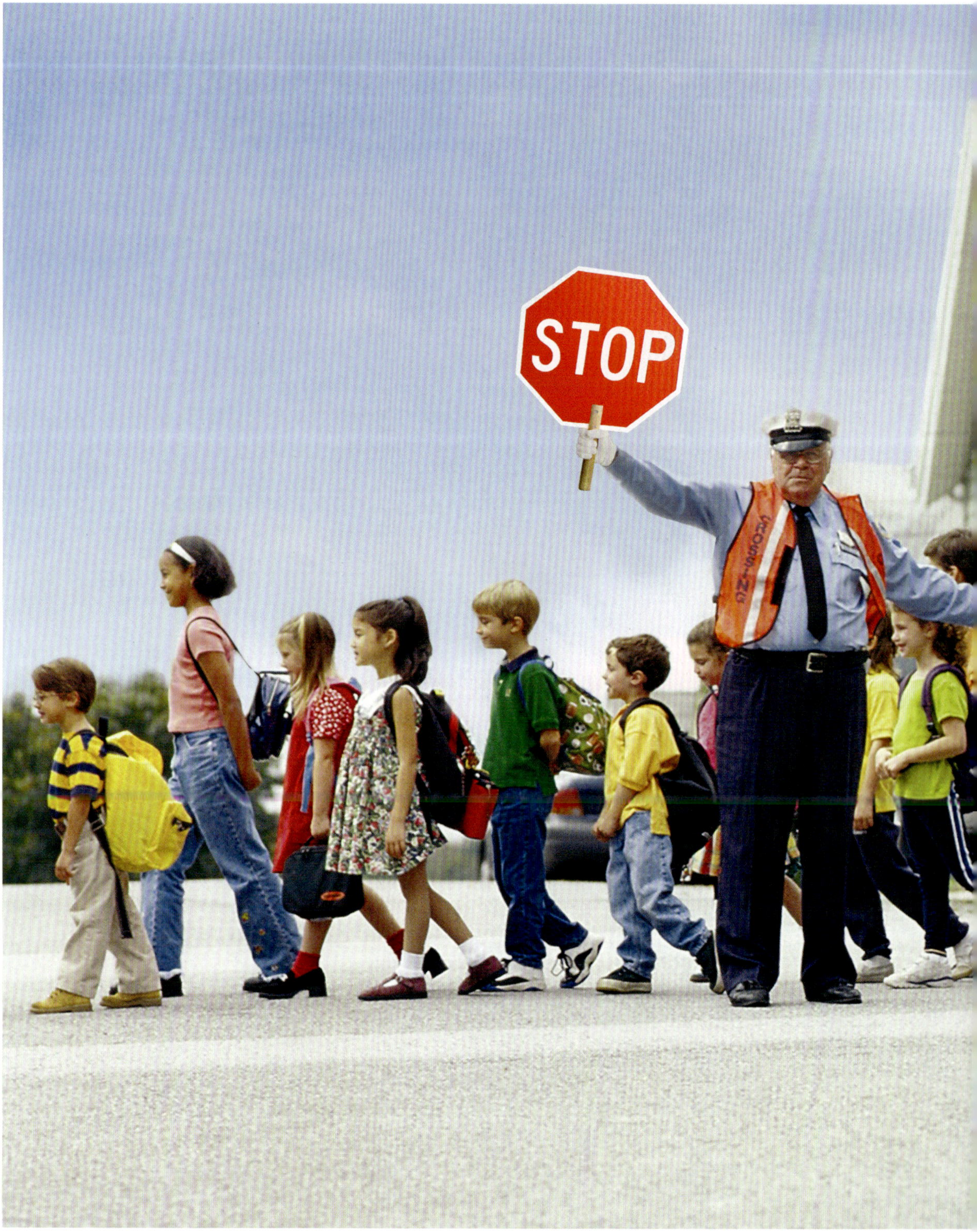
STOP
CROSSING

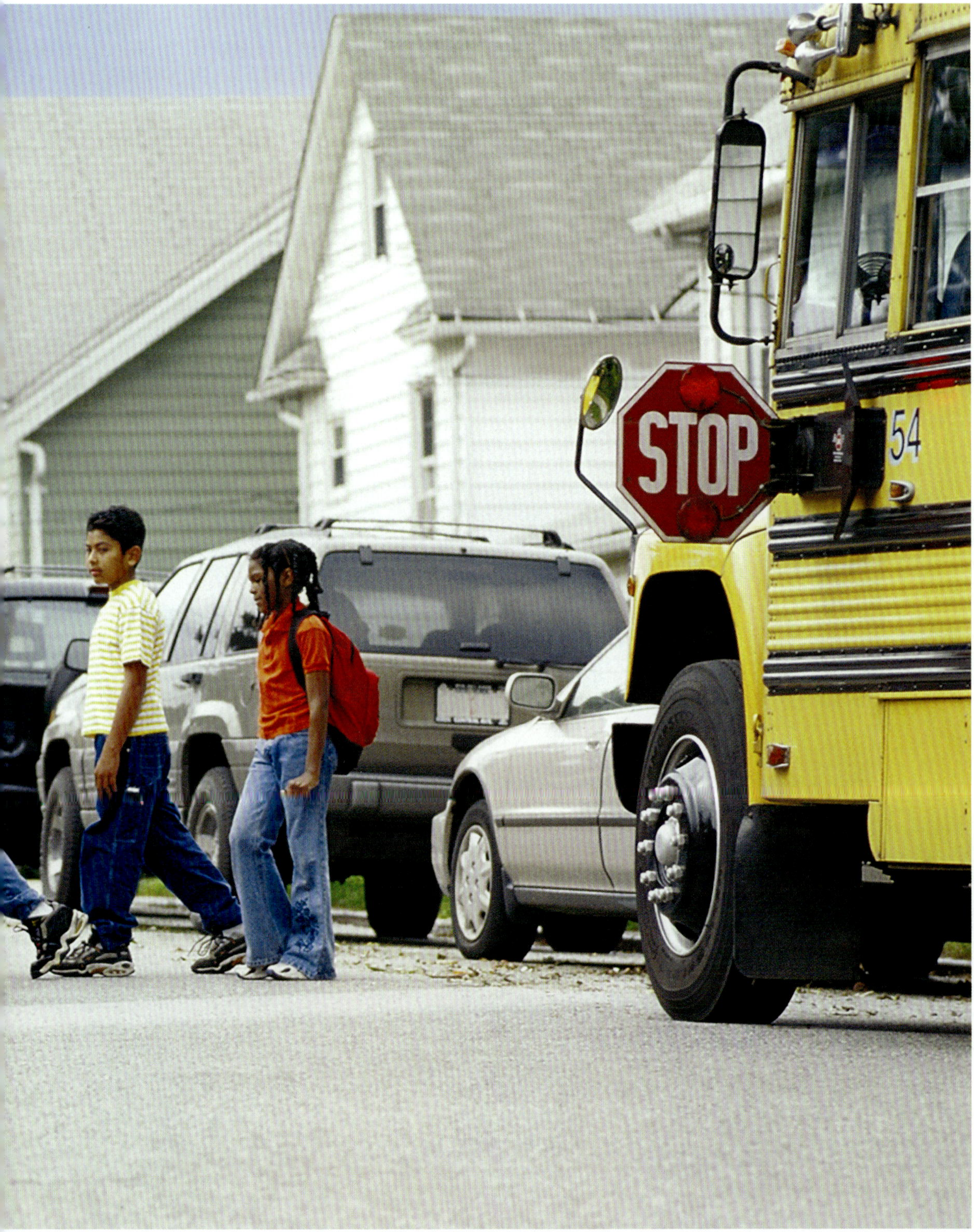
STOP
54

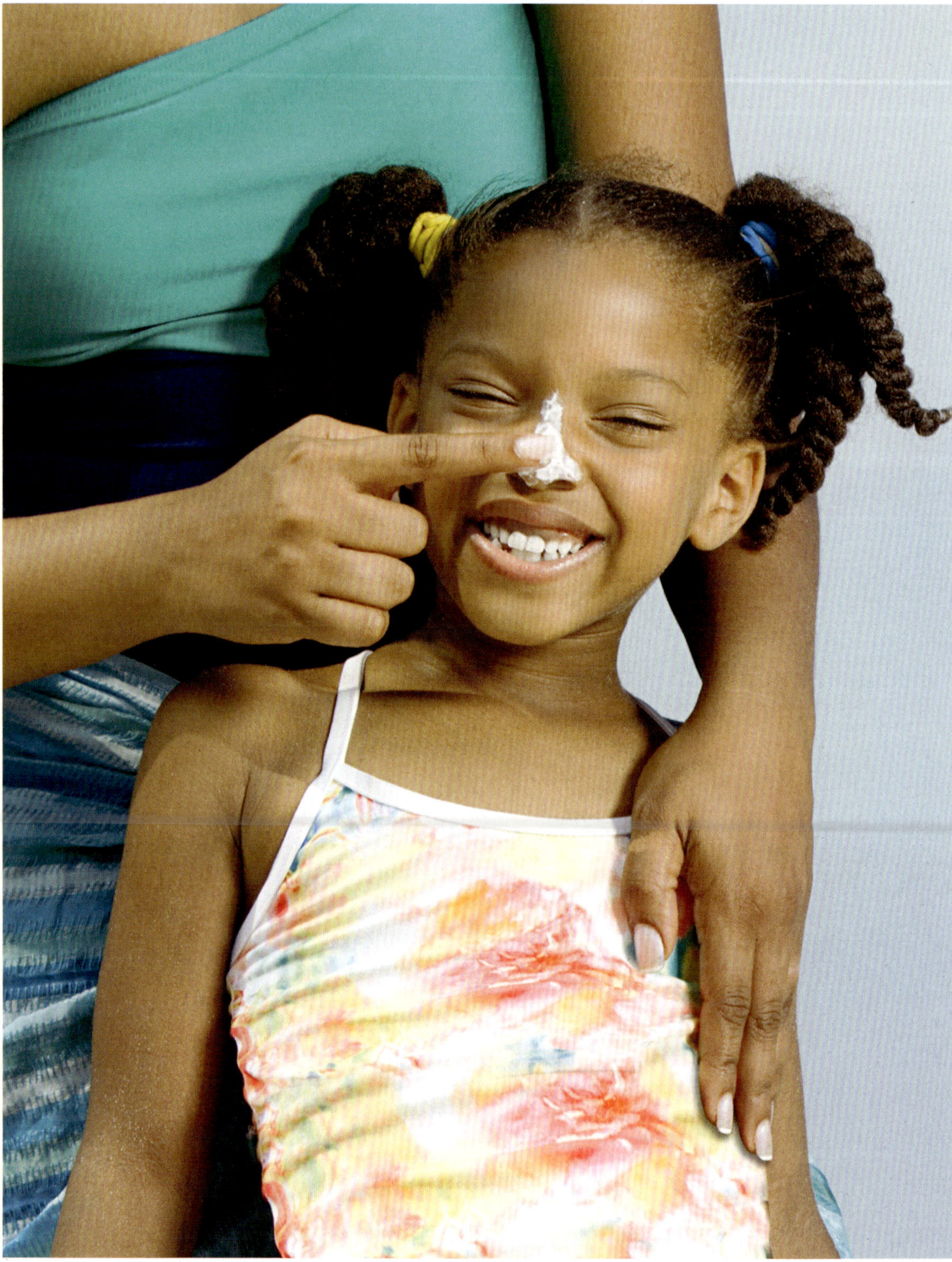

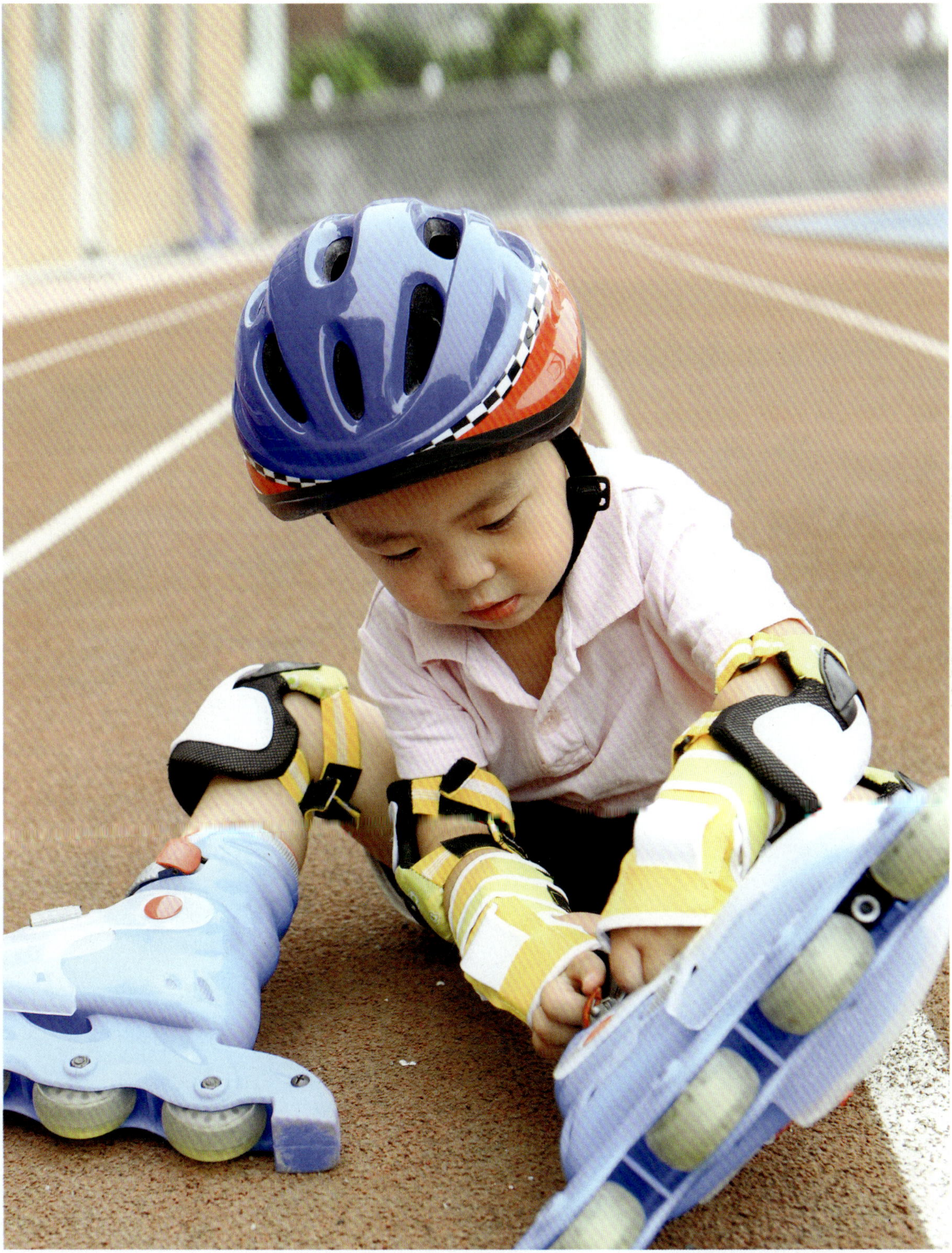

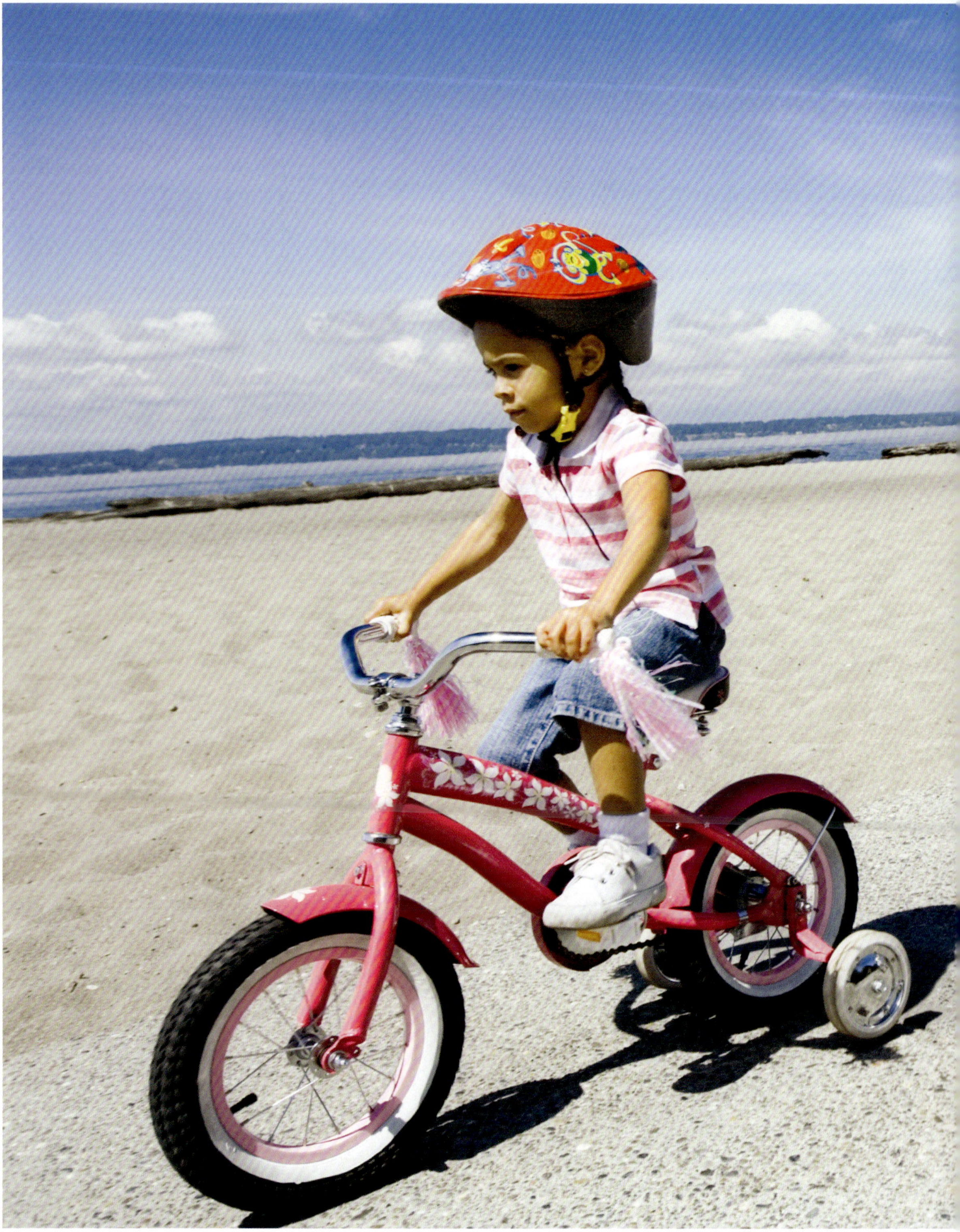

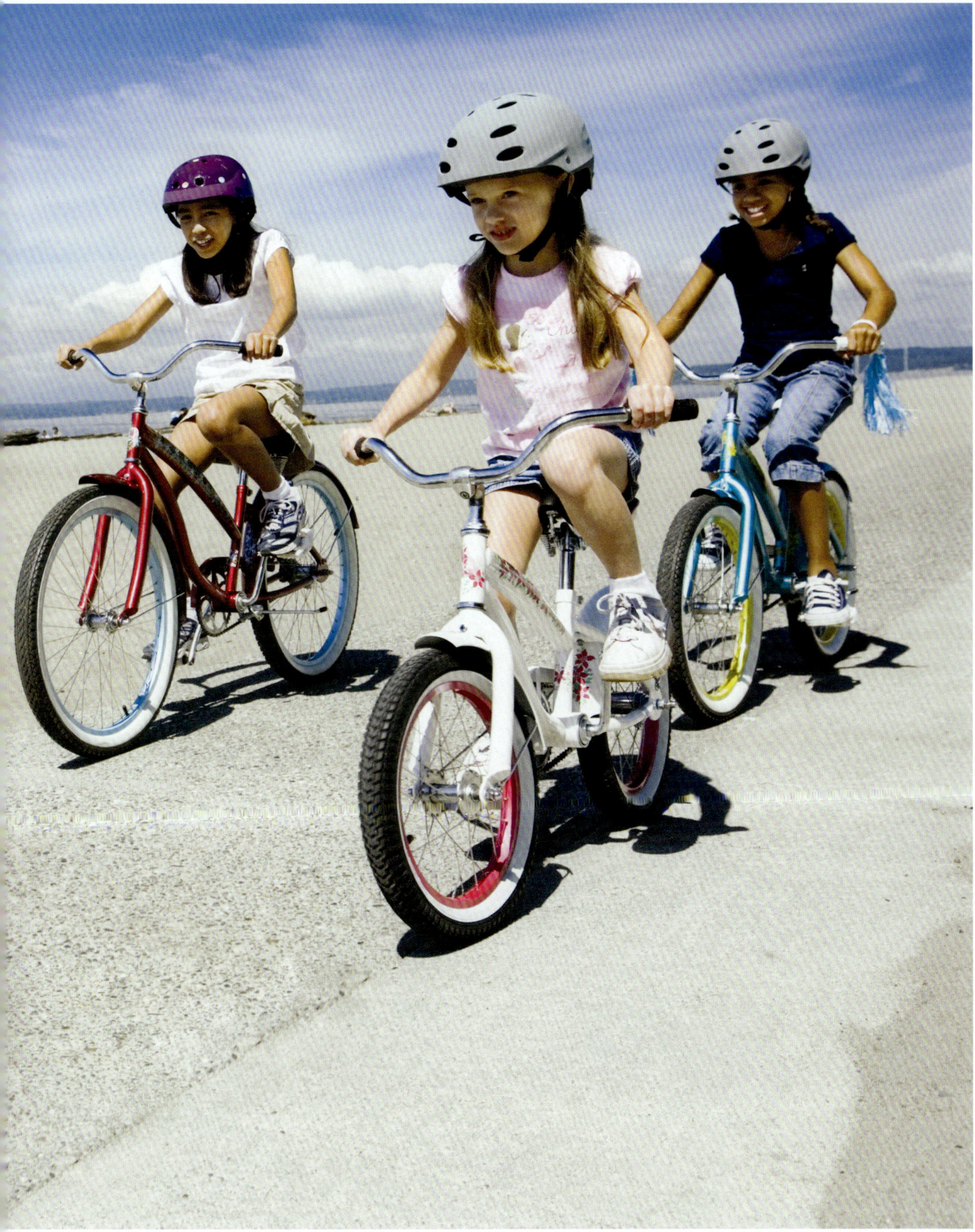

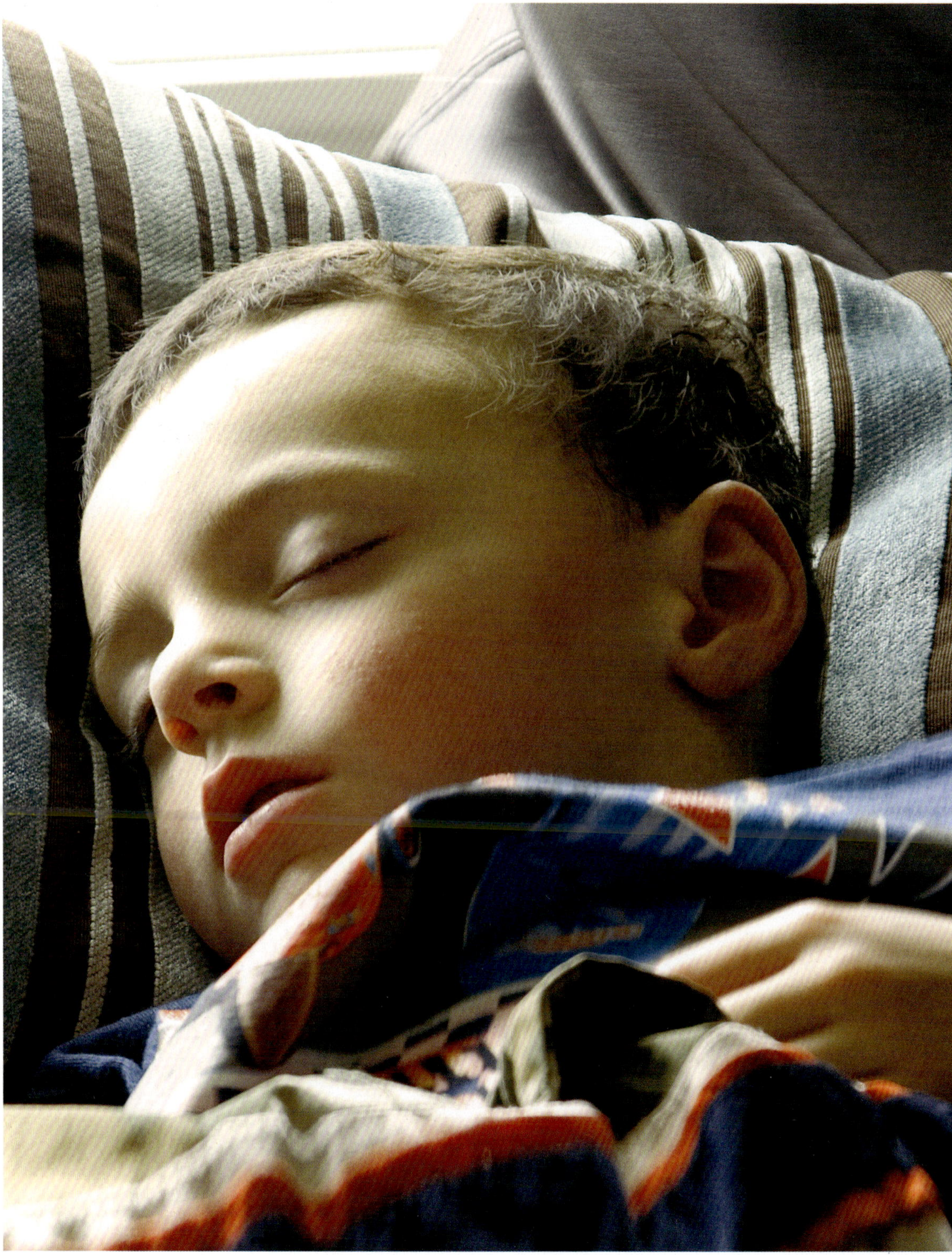